HOW TO TAKE THE
LIMITS OFF
OF
GOD

MORRIS CERULLO

Published By:

MORRIS CERULLO WORLD EVANGELISM
P.O. Box 85277, San Diego, CA 92186-5277 USA
(858) 277-2200
e-mail: morriscerullo@mcwe.com
Website: www.mcwe.com

MORRIS CERULLO WORLD EVANGELISM
P.O. Box 3600, Concord, Ontario L4K 1B6 Canada
(905) 669-1788

MORRIS CERULLO WORLD EVANGELISM
OF GREAT BRITAIN
P.O. Box 277, Hemel Hempstead, Herts HP2 7DH England

4th printing 2007
3rd printing 2002
2nd printing 1989
1st printing 1978
Copyright © 1978
Morris Cerullo World Evangelism
Printed in the U.S.A.

TABLE OF
CONTENTS

GOD KNOWS NO LIMITS

The God we serve is a God Who knows no limits. Say that out loud, right now, as you begin to read this book: The God that we serve is a God Who knows no limits! Think about what you are saying, and say it once more: The God that we serve is a God Who knows no limits!

God is unlimited, yet man limits an unlimited God. God is completely unlimited as to time or space or condition or to any concept for that matter. He is all-powerful, all-authoritative, and all-creative. Absolutely nothing is impossible to Him. There is no limit to His ability, no limit to His love, no limit to His mercy, no limit to His bountifulness, and no limit to His desire to bless His people. He is completely unlimited, yet most people—even Christians—try to limit Him. They see Him in narrow concepts.

The purpose of this book is to help you take the limits off of God that you have imposed upon Him. It will help you to cut God loose to work for you, according to His unlimited ability, not according to your limited capacity. Man is a creature so infinitely inferior to the Creator, God, that it is hard for him to imagine how he could have power with God; yet, he does!

Made from the dust of the earth, enjoying life only by the inbreathing of God, and absolutely dependent on God for all of his provision, yet man has both the power and the tendency to limit

God to the tiniest fraction of what He would and could be in that life and experience.

There are many reasons that we limit God. Many of these reasons have to do with our background or environment or upbringing. Many of them have to do with tradition. God has been presented to us within certain limits by our parents, our pastors, our teachers, our peers, and we frequently see Him only within those limits.

When we question people for information so that we will have a more solid understanding of things, we are often given vague answers, such as, "That's just the way it is," or "That's the way we do it," or "That's how we learned it." It seems that sometimes this is standard procedure in our churches and in our lives. We are told, "That's the way it has always been done," or "That's the way my grandmother did it," or "That's the tradition."

We also limit God by our experiences or our natural ability to experience God. How often I have heard people say, "Show me a miracle, and I will believe, but until then, I won't believe anything I can't see. I won't accept anything I can't touch."

There is a major reason that we limit our unlimited God. It is at the base. It is the root of all other reasons we might give. It is this: **We limit our unlimited God because we do not see Him as He really is**. *That is a very important fact.* I pray that God will remove the blinding, spiritual cataracts from your eyes, so that you will be able to see Him as He really is. It will revolutionize your life completely.

We are living in a day when God is moving by His Spirit in a tremendous way. In what we call the *charismatic movement*, we have seen the Holy Spirit sweep mightily across denominational barriers, across ethnic boundaries, and going against traditional patterns.

We have seen old-line, denominational churches open their windows for a fresh, free flow of the Holy Spirit over their congregations. We have seen congregations of literally thousands of charismatics from many different denominational backgrounds standing with their hands raised and praising God in the beautiful prayer language of the Holy Spirit. We have seen prayer for the sick and afflicted become a regular part of the program, especially in churches that were formerly closed to such activities. We have seen many, many miracles being performed, where God's Spirit has been allowed to move freely. Yet, there is so much more that God wants to do for us than what we have allowed Him to do for us.

What we have seen is just one drop of water compared to a vast ocean. It is a mere, infinitesimal speck. In spite of the great outpouring of God's Spirit that we are witnessing in our day, our churches are still filled with sick and afflicted people, with men and women and children who have problems and perplexities and burdens that are almost impossible to bear.

There are 35,000 suicides that are reported every year in the United States, with many experts believing that the actual figure is closer to 100,000. There are an estimated 15 million alcoholics who are seeking answers to their problems in the depths of a whiskey bottle. There are more than 5,000 drug-related deaths each year. The divorce rate has reached nearly one out of every two marriages in North America. I could go on and on. Yet, the whole time these tragedies are taking place, there is a limitless God, Who is in charge of this universe, and Who is ready, willing, and able to meet every need that mankind has. **Every** need!

It is not only the heathen or the unchurched whose needs are not being met. Many good, Bible-believing, church-attending Christians are enduring a multitude of difficulties. I wish you could see a portion of the mail that comes into my office every week. There are astounding needs, overwhelming needs—financial, mental, emotional, spiritual, familial, physical—yet there is not one need that a person can name that God is not able to meet. People just need to learn how to take the limits off of God. If they could just see Him as He really is, and cut Him loose to do what He is able to do and wants to do for them, they would see their entire lives and circumstances in a different light.

In many places where God is moving, and people are seeing many answers to prayer, they rejoice in what has been done (and rightly so), but they fail to see how much more God has for those who will open their lives to Him completely. Many churches and individuals have limited God to the point of blessing that they have received up to the present time, and they develop a certain sense of smugness with it. They think they "have it," or that they "have arrived." Some people, some churches, and some denominations think that they have seen all that God has for them, but nothing could be farther from the truth.

If what we see in the churches today is representative of all that God is, and if what we see in the churches today is representative of the power of the resurrected Christ, then the world is in deep trouble!

I am convinced that God wants to burst out of the limits that we have put Him under and that He yearns to manifest His unlimited ability in our lives in a way that we have not dreamed could be possible. We have seen a little of His miracle-working power, but I am convinced that we have not seen anything yet, compared to what God wants to do and what He will do, as we cut Him loose to work, according to His own ability.

Eighteen years ago, God told me that we have not seen anything yet and that greater miracles are still to come. I was just a young preacher of 28 years old. I was in the Philippine Islands for a crusade that continued for three breathtaking weeks because of what the Holy Spirit was doing. On the last day of the crusade, we baptized more than 1,200 people in water, in one of the largest water baptismal services that was ever recorded on the foreign field in one day. It took 50 National ministers (all baptizing people at the same time) to get the job done.

We went from that baptismal service to Roxas park, across the street from the city hall building in Manila, where about 30,000 people were present for the closing service. In spite of the glow from the baptismal service we had just been in, and in spite of the great number of people who were packed together in the huge park for this service, one, single, individual person in that vast crowd stood out like a light.

We had ropes all around the front of the crowd to keep the area directly in front of the platform clear. Right behind the rope, sitting on the ground, was the worst, most twisted, emaciated mess of a man that I have ever seen. He looked awful, what you might call a hopeless case. I had been preaching only about ten minutes when God began to do an amazing thing. Before my eyes, this terribly crippled man began to get up. His bones began to break loose and pop and jerk, until they came completely untwisted, and he began to walk right there in front of the huge crowd in the open space in front of the platform!

As people began to see what was happening to this wreck of a man, there was a shocked instant of stunned silence, and then holy bedlam broke loose. It was holy bedlam, for God was surely in it. I never saw such a sight. All over that park, mothers began to pick up their little, crippled children and set them on their feet. These were children who had never walked in their lives. The mothers were saying to them, "In the Name of Jesus, WALK!" The children would fall to the ground, and the mothers would pick them up, stand them on their feet, and again command them to walk in the Name of Jesus. The children would again fall, and the mothers would again pick them up, and again command them to walk in Jesus' Name a second and third time. They were commanding their children over and over and over, until the little children not only were walking but were running around in that open space! Scores of them were running around! In no time at all, the entire area was filled with children who had been crippled, but who now were walking and running all over the place. They filled the platform with all kinds of walking sticks, canes, and crutches. There must have been a pile—at least two feet high—consisting of every kind of brace, stick, or crutch you could possibly imagine.

I was standing there, watching this great display of God's power, and I began to weep. I was so completely overcome that I ran off of that platform and hid behind it. I took hold of a post and just began to weep and to cry out to God. I cried, "Lord, just take me home. Just take me home. I don't want to live any more. No one should see this much of Your glory and live!" I was holding onto the post, crying out to God, and weeping, when a big, tall minister (one of the missionaries there in the Philippines) came to me, put his arm around me, and said, "Brother Cerullo, you had better get back to the platform, and take charge of this meeting, or we are going to have a riot on our hands."

I went back up the ramp to the wooden platform that had been erected for the services. I looked at the work of God that was still going on. I saw the tremendous outpouring of the Holy Spirit, and I said, "God, how can I control this? There isn't anything that I can do to control it!" That is when God spoke to me, as clearly as you speak to your friends, unmistakably and clearly. He said, "Son, you haven't seen anything yet!" I will never forget it.

I believe that this is where we are today. We are seeing an outpouring of God's Spirit. We are receiving the blessing. We are seeing a measure of His glory, so much so that sometimes we are nearly overcome with it all. But we haven't seen anything yet!

The Church was born in a great demonstration of apostolic power. It was not brought into being by great orators or because of great preaching. It was born by a demonstration of the power of the Holy Spirit. Paul, one of the greatest preachers in all of history, was a brilliant man and an educated man, yet this is what he had to say about the results that he had for God: . . . *my speech and my preaching was not with enticing words of man's wisdom, but in demonstration of the Spirit and of power:* (1 Corinthians 2:4). It wasn't what he **said** as much as what he **showed**.

The greatest lack in the Church today is power. God told us to have power. We have teachings, we have tongues, we have blessings, but we have not seen the power that God wants to unleash in and through our lives. Jesus said: *Behold, I give unto you power to tread on serpents and scorpions, and over all the power of the enemy: and nothing shall by any means hurt you* (Luke 10:19). He said: *But ye shall receive power, after that the Holy Ghost is come upon you: and ye shall be witnesses unto me both in Jerusalem, and in all Judaea, and in Samaria, and unto the uttermost part of the earth* (Acts 1:8). He said: *And these signs shall follow them that believe; In my name shall they cast out devils; they shall speak with new tongues; They shall take up serpents; and if they drink any deadly thing, it shall not hurt them; they shall lay hands on the sick, and they shall recover* (Mark 16:17-18).

We haven't seen anything yet! In Ephesians, Paul wrote a letter under the inspiration of the Holy Spirit. He said, *Now unto him that is able to do exceeding abundantly above all that we ask or think, according to the power that worketh in us,* (Ephesians 3:20). The Church has entered into a place of great blessing, but it has failed to press into the place of **power** that God has for it. It has stopped far short of its potential.

I prophesy to you that Jesus is coming back soon! I also prophesy that the Church will be raptured in a greater demonstration of power than it was born in, and it was born in a great outpouring of the Holy Spirit, accompanied by apostolic miracles that literally . . . *turned the world upside down* . . . (Acts 17:6). We will begin to see that power and demonstration in our lives, in our own ministries, and in our churches when we begin to see God as He really is, when we see the limitlessness and the power that He wants to impart to us, and when give Him the freedom to work in our lives.

One of the greatest stories of a miracle in the Bible is the one that speaks of a man who saw Jesus as He really is. Before we turn to his experience, as an example of what God can and will do for us, I want to pray this very special prayer for you, so that you will be free to receive all that God would have you to receive from these words.

Right now, I want you to place your hand on this page and upon your Bible as a point of contact, and absorb into your very being what God wants to do for you, as you receive this ministry right now:

Heavenly Father, I come to You in the Name of Jesus Christ, the Name that is above every name. I ask You to loose every spiritual cataract that is blinding the eyes of every person who is reading these words. Let those blinding cataracts fall off and be gone. Let spiritual vision and insight be anointed and quickened as never before. In Jesus' Name I come against, and I bind, every hindering thought, every doubt, every preoccupation, and every diversion in this mind and life and spirit right now. I loose upon this heart and mind the spirit of liberty and clarity and understanding of Who You are. Let the Holy Ghost revelation break forth with light upon every word as it is read. Let this life be one that, in this very hour, comes to see Jesus as He really is, and in doing so, may every limitation of Your power in this life be completely destroyed and banished, that You might be cut loose to do a work of miracles and might, such as we have never witnessed. Do a new thing in this individual's life and heart right now, in Jesus' Name. Amen.

IS THERE A "DAY OF MIRACLES"?

We are going now to a miracle story in the Bible, which contains one of the greatest miracles that ever happened in the life and ministry of Jesus Christ on earth. From it, we can learn a great lesson in how to cut God loose to work in our lives beyond our meager human abilities. He will be free to work according to His unlimited abilities. The story is found in Matthew 8:5-13:

And when Jesus was entered into Capernaum, there came unto him a centurion, beseeching him, And saying, Lord, my servant lieth home sick of the palsy, grievously tormented. And Jesus saith unto him, I will come and heal him. The centurion answered and said, Lord, I am not worthy that thou shouldest come under my roof: but speak the word only, and my servant shall be healed. For I am a man under authority, having soldiers under me: and I say to this man, Go, and he goeth; and to another, Come, and he cometh; and to my servant, Do this, and he doeth it. When Jesus heard it, he marvelled, and said to them that followed, Verily I say unto you, I have not found so great faith, no, not in Israel. And I say unto you, That many shall come from the east and west, and shall sit down with Abraham, and Isaac, and Jacob, in the kingdom of heaven. But the children of the kingdom shall be cast out into outer darkness: there shall be weeping and gnashing of teeth. And Jesus said unto the centurion, Go thy way; and as thou hast believed, so be it done unto thee. And his servant was healed in the selfsame hour.

Many people say to me, "Brother Cerullo, that might have happened in Bible days, but the days of miracles have past." They say, "Those things were just for Bible days or just for the apostolic age." There are several things I want to tell you in this regard. The first is that there is no such thing as a day of miracles. Such a thing has never existed. **There is no such thing as a day of miracles or days of miracles; there is only a God of miracle-working power, and He does not change!** He is just as capable to do miracles today as He was in any age that has ever existed. Men change. Denominations change. Styles change. God never changes.

When the children of Israel were crying out to God for deliverance from the great bondage they were under in Egypt, God chose Moses to go and represent Him before Pharaoh, and lead the Israelites out of Egypt. Moses was a fugitive. He had left Israel following the taunting by his own countrymen (as well as the threats of the Egyptians) to report him for killing two Egyptians that were beating some Hebrew men. The Israelites didn't trust him, and the Egyptians wanted to kill him. Moses fled to the back side of the desert and made a new life for himself there. He became a herdsman. He got married and had a family.

God never forgot about Moses or how He was going to use his life. One day, Moses saw a strange sight in the desert. He saw a bush that was on fire but wasn't being burned up. When Moses turned aside to see this strange sight, he found out that it was God. God was trying to get Moses' attention and trying to get him to cut God loose to work in and through his life. He had left Egypt in disgrace and fear. Now, here was God commanding him to go back and stand before Pharaoh and become the deliverer of Israel. Moses was understandably shaken by all of this. *And Moses said unto God, Behold, when I come unto the children of Israel, and shall say unto them, The God of your fathers hath sent me unto you; and they shall say to me, What is his name? what shall I say unto them?* (Exodus 3:13).

Moses knew better than to go in his own name. They would throw him out. They would never listen. He knew that he needed more authority than that. He may have been thinking, God, they will want to know where I got this authority to come back and take charge. What shall I tell them? Whom shall I tell them sent me? I can't go in my name. Whose name am I going in? The name that God gave Moses to describe Himself is the most powerful, most potent expression of the ability and nature of God that could possibly be put into English words: *And God said unto Moses, I AM THAT I AM: and he said, Thus shalt thou say unto the children of Israel, I AM hath sent me unto you* (Exodus 3:14).

God didn't say, I was, or I will be. He said, *I AM*. He is the God of NOW. He is the ever-present, the ever-able, and the very epitome of timelessness and limitlessness. **I AM**. God is **I AM**. He proved Himself as *I AM* in Moses' day, when He brought the children of Israel out of Egypt with a mighty arm and wrought great miracles of deliverance on their behalf. Not only did He bring great plagues upon the Egyptians to make them willing to let the children of Israel go free, but His watchful care and protection of the Israelites after they left Egypt was miraculous. Every step of the way that they took in the wilderness, God was there.

They crossed the sea on dry land. They drank water out of a rock. Their food was rained down upon them from heaven on a daily basis. Their clothing did not get old. Their shoes did not wear out. So great was God's care that there was not one feeble person among them. God led them with a cloud during the day and with a pillar of fire at night. Talk about a day of miracles. There were new miracles being done by God for them every day.

Moses later died. This event caused the mantle of leadership to fall upon Joshua. God said to Joshua, Now I want you to lead Israel and perform the miracles. Joshua could barely believe it. He said, God, you know I can't do miracles. I'm just the general of the army.

Moses was the miracle worker, and he's gone. When he was here, it was the day of miracles, but now Moses is gone. His day of miracles is past. Joshua continued, God, I didn't lead the children out of Egypt. Moses did. I didn't open the Red Sea. You used Moses to do those things. I didn't feed the children of Israel. Moses did.

Joshua thought the day of miracles was past now that Moses— God's chosen and anointed servant for a certain ministry—was gone. But God had not changed. God was not dead. He was just the same as He had been when Moses was alive. God said, Joshua, I want to tell you something. Moses didn't do any of those things that you just said he did. I did them. **I AM THAT I AM**! I revealed Myself in the pillar of cloud by day and in the pillar of fire by night. It wasn't Moses' rod that opened the Red Sea. I did that. It wasn't Moses who sent the manna from heaven for you to eat. I sent it. It wasn't Moses who made water pour out of a rock when you were thirsty. I did it. It wasn't Moses. It wasn't his rod. It wasn't his "day." I am the One Who did these miracles. I am just as much with you now as I was with Moses then. Now, Joshua, if you will pick up that ark, and march out, and dare to stand on my Word, which I am speaking to you now, then you will find that **I AM** is still here and that My miracle-working power is still here, even though Moses is gone.

Moses' day was past, but God's was not. It IS not. God's day is still here and always will be. *For I am the LORD, I change not . . .* (Malachi 3:6). *Every good gift and every perfect gift is from above, and cometh down from the Father of lights, with whom is no variableness, neither shadow of turning* (James 1:17).

There have been miracles in every day and in every age that men and women have dared to believe God and act on His Word. The miracles were not according to the natural abilities of mankind, but according to the power and unlimited ability of God.

The Book of Daniel recounts the story of three Hebrew children that were thrown into a fiery furnace for refusing to bow down and worship the king of Babylon. They might have feared the power of the furnace or of losing their lives from the heat or the flames. They might have said, Well, we are surely going to perish, for only a miracle can save us, and miracles were only for Moses' day. But they didn't say that. They said, . . . *our God . . . is able to deliver us . . .* (Daniel 3:17).

When they were thrown into the fiery furnace for their trust in God, there appeared a fourth figure walking around in the furnace with them that was described as being . . . *like the Son of God* (Daniel 3:25). The three Hebrew men came out of the furnace unscathed and unburned. Not a hair of their heads was singed. Their clothes did not even have the smell of smoke in them. The God of miracles was present in their day (Daniel 3:17-26).

When the sons of the prophets were cutting down trees to build a new dwelling place in the time of Elisha, one of them had borrowed an axe. As he was chopping, the axe head flew off and went into the river. When he told Elisha what had happened, Elijah didn't say, Well, it's no use. Elijah isn't here any more. Elijah is the one who used to work miracles. His day was the day of miracles, but he is gone now.

Elisha didn't say that because he **knew** that it wasn't Elijah who did the miracles. It was God! He asked, Where did the axe head fall? Here, throw a stick in. When the stick was thrown into the water, God turned it into a magnet, and the axe head rose to the top of the water and floated (2 Kings 6:5-6), because **that** day was a miracle day!

Elisha had a greater understanding than most people about the so-called *day of miracles.* I am sure that he appreciated the ministry of Elijah and that he loved him dearly. When Elijah was taken up and received into heaven in a miraculous way, Elisha didn't just sit down, cry, and say, Well, I guess it's all over. Elijah's gone. I guess I had better get back to my plowing. No. He picked up Elijah's mantle, struck the water with it, and boldly demanded, . . . *Where is the Lord God of Elijah? . . .*

(2 Kings 2:14). He didn't ask where Elijah was, but where was the **Lord God** of Elijah.

Elisha knew Who had performed the miracles. He knew it wasn't a day of miracles or even a man of miracles. It was the GOD of miracles. Elisha found Him just as present in his own life and ministry as He had been in Elijah's. God doesn't need men in order to work miracles. He doesn't need human instruments to work through, though He often does. He can work through even the dumbest animal, as we can see when we read the account of Balaam in Numbers 22:21-35 in the Old Testament.

The heathen king, Balak, sent a committee to bribe the prophet Balaam to come and curse the children of Israel. Balaam angered God by starting out with these men on his donkey. Once, twice, and then a third time, an angel waited along the trail to slay Balaam in God's wrath, but each time, the donkey balked, and Balaam's life was saved. Balaam had not seen the angel waiting to slay him. He got angry at the donkey and began beating him. God used the donkey to do a miracle. The donkey began to talk to Balaam. Donkeys don't talk, but that one did, because the God of miracles was on the scene in **that** day.

God was the **I AM** in Enoch's day. A miracle translated Enoch out of this world because Enoch walked with God (Hebrews 11:5).

The God of miracles was on the scene in Abraham's day. A son of promise was born to someone that the Bible describes as being *as good as dead* with respect to their ability to father a child (Hebrews 11:11-12).

The God of miracles was present in Samson's day, when Samson slew 1,000 Philistines with the jawbone of an ass (Judges 15:15-16).

The God of miracles was there when a great host of angels encompassed the city that Elisha was in, where he was surrounded by enemies who were seeking to kill him (2 Kings 6:8-23).

The God of miracles was present in Daniel's day, when Daniel was thrown into a den with hungry lions (Daniel 6:16-22).

The God of miracles was present when a widow's small cruse of oil, and an even smaller supply of meal, miraculously lasted throughout an entire famine (1 Kings 17:8-16).

The Old Testament is full of miracles, but all of them are miracles of God. They are not miracles of a day of miracles.

There is no such thing as an "apostolic age" of miracles, such as many church people call the miracles wrought through Peter, James, John, Paul, and other New Testament individuals. Not a single apostle of those days made any claims in scripture about an apostolic age or apostolic day.

Many churches and denominations read in the Book of Acts about the outpouring of the Holy Spirit and the miracles wrought by the hands of the apostles, and they miss the point entirely. They say that that was "for their day," or that "that day is past." There is nothing in the Word of God to even suggest that God gave the Church something "for that day" (to get it off to a good start) and then withdrew it.

In fact, speaking of the outpouring of God's Holy Spirit, Peter said: *For the promise is unto you, and to your children, and to all that are afar off, even as many as the Lord our God shall call* (Acts 2:39). The apostles never even kept records of their acts. Very little is recorded in the Bible about the things that God used them to accomplish. Most of what was recorded was written by Luke, a physician who was not even an apostle.

Even if there was such a thing as an apostolic day or an apostolic age, it would not be over, for God means for the Church today to have apostles in it. *And he gave some, apostles; and some, prophets; and some, evangelists; and some, pastors and teachers; For the perfecting of the saints, for the work of the ministry, for the edifying of the body of Christ* (Ephesians 4:11-12).

The reason we are not taking the world for Christ today is that we are mainly employing and emphasizing the ministries of pastors and teachers. We are neglecting to develop and honor and expect the other ministry gifts to be present, operating and being used in the Church body.

Feeding Christians and teaching them the Word of God is needed, and it is important. However, many times it only serves to make the Church spiritually fat, and it is not being translated into action, into working miracles, into reaching the lost, and into setting people free. These are what should be the normal outreach of a Spirit-filled congregation. Pastors and teachers are not the basic military gifts that will break the walls of satanic power and open our cities to the power of God.

To do the work of God in these last days, it will take apostolic power in **this** age, not in some other age. We must look to the day of NOW and in US, not in Peter, not in Paul, and not in a day of apostles. God has put in the Church **apostles**. This is the apostolic age. The miracle-working God is still on the throne of the universe.

There are many theologians who do not claim that the day of miracles is past. In fact, they claim that there never was such a thing as a day of miracles. They will go to great lengths and impossible theories and colorful rhetoric to explain away any miracle recorded in the Bible or any that they may hear about today.

They explain away the burning bush that Moses saw in the desert and the crossing of the Red Sea on dry land. They explain that 5,000 people were fed with two loaves and five fishes because loaves of bread were bigger in that day, but they forget that one little boy was carrying those loaves. They also claim that there must have been fewer people there, but the reality is that there were more people. The 5,000 were only the men that were there. The Bible says that in addition to this number of men, there were also women and children present. They, of course, also claim that Jonah was not really swallowed by a whale.

They can give a natural reason for how a victim of incurable cancer inexplicably recovers after prayer, or tell you that the lions that were in the den with Daniel were well fed before Daniel got in there, but they forget to tell you how the lions devoured Daniel's accusers. They don't believe in miracles now, and they don't believe in miracles in the past. They say there has never been a day of miracles.

I have absolutely no doctrinal argument with them at all on that last statement. I also deny the day of miracles. I never try to prove doctrinally that there was such a day. My answer has always been that there is no day of miracles and that there never has been, but there IS an ever-present God of miracles! The datelessness of God's power is demonstrated clearly in the conversation that Jesus had with Martha at Bethany when her brother Lazarus died (John 11:1-45).

Jesus had heard that Lazarus was sick, but He didn't go to Lazarus's bedside and heal him. Jesus stayed where He was for two more days. When He finally did get to Bethany, Lazarus was dead and had been in the tomb for four days. His sister, Martha, upbraided Jesus for not having come home immediately. She blamed Him and told Him that if He had been there, her brother would not have died. In other words, she was saying, I have seen You do miracles of healing, and if You had come home before Lazarus died, if You had come in the past, You could have done a miracle and could have prevented him from dying!

Jesus told her that her brother would rise again. Martha's reply this time was that she knew Lazarus would rise again in the resurrection at the last day. In effect, she was saying, Lord, I know You could work miracles in the past, and I believe that You will work miracles in the future, but this is now! Yesterday was the day of miracles, and there will be miracles at some point in the future, but what about today?

Jesus set the record perfectly straight. He said, I AM the Resurrection! The resurrection life, the power of God, was on the scene in the now—not just for the past and not just for the future—and it is on the scene for today's now.

It is so sad and strange that the churches of today have to look back at what God has done in the past or look forward to a revival or move of God that they believe may come at some undetermined time in the future. God is here now, and He wants to move now. Oh, that we would open our eyes!

The only reason God does not or cannot do greater works than what we see in this day is that we have limited Him by our thinking, our attitude, and our unbelief. God has not changed. Denominations have changed. The major denominations of our day were not born spiritually cold and apathetic. They drifted into lukewarm apostasy. Churches were not born spiritually dead. They slowly drifted toward spiritual death. They were not born lukewarm. They were born alive, in the heat of the fire of God, in faith! They died through too much organization and through cold, dead theology and intellectualism, through forms, rituals, and the traditions of men!

When the Church was born, it had no forms. It had no candles to light. It had no stained-glass windows. It had no rituals. People who loved and served God simply gathered together to worship Him in Spirit and in truth. They worshiped freely and openly.

John Wesley didn't need a polished wood pulpit. He would find an open field and begin to minister with the anointing of God. When asked to explain how it was that crowds of people would come to hear him preach to the trees in the woods and thus be converted because of his burning message, he would say, "I set myself on fire, and people come out to see me burn."

It was the fire of passion for the souls of men and women that brought revival to Scotland in the 1800s, resulting in the founding of the Presbyterian Church, that caused John Knox to cry out, "Give me Scotland, or I die . . . "

It was the fire—not cold, dead theology—that made Whitefield's messages so powerful that his hearers would fall out of their seats trembling and would repent on their knees in the aisles.

There are many others that I could enumerate, such as: Luther, Calvin, Goforth, Hudson Taylor, Moody, Mueller, Wigglesworth, and so forth. Every great move of God started with a fire that was shut up in somebody's bones. I believe that this age is going to witness even greater fire and demonstration of God's power than the world has ever seen or known, as we catch a glimpse of the God of might and miracles.

God did not have a day of miracles or an age of miracles. He is the God of miracles in our day. Remember, there is no day of miracles. There is only an ever-present, never-changing God of miracle-working power!

THREE

HOW CAN WE KNOW GOD'S WILL?

One of the greatest limitations that we put on God is not knowing what His will is for us. People are prone to saying, Well, I believe God works miracles today when it is His **will**, or God could heal me if He wanted to, but it must be His **will** for me to suffer or to go through this.

One thing that always struck me as odd was someone who said that it was God's will for them to be sick, but then spent hundreds of dollars on medicine and doctors and hospitals trying to **get out** of God's will, instead of **accepting** "God's will," and carrying the pain, sickness, and need, giving God the glory for it and **not** trying to get rid of His will!

Let me assure you here and now that **it is not God's will for you to be sick**. It is not God's will for you to suffer. It is not God's will for you to go hungry or threadbare. It is God's will to bless you and meet every need that you have. It **is** His will that you live in a place of health and happiness and abundance. *Beloved, I wish above all things that thou mayest prosper and be in health, even as thy soul prospereth* (3 John 2).

When the centurion approached Jesus, he had an urgent request. His servant, whom he loved dearly, was lying at home, sick with palsy. Palsy is a complete or partial muscle paralysis, often accompanied by a loss of sensation and uncontrollable body movements or tremors. That affliction was not just a nervous shaking and constant deterioration as we know it today. That is bad enough. This man was wholly and totally paralyzed. Also, as the centurion said, he was grievously tormented and in great pain at all times.

I am sure that the centurion had sought help for his beloved servant everywhere he could. Somehow, in his search, he came to find out about Jesus and His miracle-working power. The centurion's faith was triggered. He turned to Jesus for help. When Jesus heard the request, His immediate response was: I will come and heal him!

I WILL! The will of God is something that we need to know more about because there is no way that you can have faith for healing or any other miracle if you do not believe that it is God's will to heal you or to give you that miracle. It was the will of God for the centurion's servant to be healed. It is the will of God today to heal you and to heal your loved ones. You cannot change the will of God. You cannot change the will of any person after they are dead.

Before Jesus left this earth, He plainly declared what His will is and what He was leaving for us. He accomplished His mission here on earth, and this purpose is stated clearly in 1 John 3:8: . . . *For this purpose the Son of God was manifested, that he might destroy the works of the devil.* His will is declared in Matthew 8:17: . . . *Himself took our infirmities, and bare our sicknesses.*

It is God's will for us to have prosperity and health, and it is as important for us to know that it is His will for us to have these things as it is to know that He is able to give us these things. It is God's will to save every person from their sins. *The Lord is not slack concerning his promise, as some men count slackness; but is longsuffering to us-ward, not willing that any should perish, but that all should come to repentance* (2 Peter 3:9). *All that the father giveth me shall come to me; and him that cometh to me I will in no wise cast out* (John 6:37). *But as many as received him, to them gave he power to become the sons of God, even to them that believe on his name:* (John 1:12).

As it is God's will to heal the soul, to forgive sins, and to remove the guilt of those sins, it is also God's will to heal everyone who is sick and afflicted. *Who his own self bare our sins in his own body on the tree, that we, being dead to sins, should live unto righteousness: by whose stripes ye were healed* (1 Peter 2:24).

Let me repeat that. **It is God's will to heal everyone who is sick.** That is a big statement, and it may make some of you shake your head a little in disbelief, but it is true. The main reason today that so many people remain in their sickness and in their afflictions is that they do not and cannot believe that it is God's will to heal them.

Many of our denominational friends, many churches, and many theologians want to change the will of God. They say and teach that it is not God's will to heal today. Their theology does not change what Christ bought and paid for. It only changes what people believe about it. Many people in our churches today, and many ministers, have been conditioned to believe that healing is not for our day. They have grown up with that teaching, and it is sometimes hard to lose.

Not many days prior to the writing of this message, a very prominent, nationwide, Sunday morning television program featured a speaker on it. The speaker went on at length about how healing is not for today and how the day of miracles is past. At the end of the program, this man invited his viewers to write to him so that he could pray for them. I wonder if he realized the great contradictions within his own presentation. How could that man pray in faith for answers to prayer when he had just spent so much time explaining why God doesn't answer prayers today?

THE PRAYER OF FAITH

We can never pray the prayer of faith for anything until we know that what we are praying for is God's will. The prayer of faith must be tied to infallibility. Infallibility means that it cannot be questioned. We must know beyond question that it is God's will to heal us if we are going to pray in faith. We can pray and know that something will happen when we know that we are tied to that which cannot be questioned. The only thing in the world that is infallible, which cannot be questioned, is God's Word. It is not just His written Word, the Bible, but it is also the living Word, which is Jesus. Everything that has ever been created was created by God's Word.

. . . God said, Let there be light: and there was light (Genesis 1:3). *And God said, . . . let the dry land appear: and it was so* (Genesis 1:9). *And God said, Let the earth bring forth . . . and it was so* (Genesis 1:11). Every time God spoke for something to happen, it happened. It happened because of the creative power of God's Word. It could not be questioned. It was infallible. Out of nothing, God created everything that was created by the power of His infallible Word.

That was His spoken Word. The living Word was also there the whole time. *IN the beginning was the Word, and the Word was with God, and the Word was God. The same was in the beginning with God. All things were made by him; and without him was not any thing made that was made. And the Word was made flesh, and dwelt among us, (and we beheld his glory, the glory as of the only begotten of the Father,) full of grace and truth* (John 1:1-2,14).

God's Word is truth: *. . . God, that cannot lie, promised . . .* (Titus 1:2). *. . . it was impossible for God to lie . . .* (Hebrews 6:18). *Jesus said, . . . I am the way, the truth, and the life . . .* (John 14:6). *Forever, O LORD, thy word is settled in heaven* (Psalms 119:89). It cannot and will not ever be changed. *Heaven and earth shall pass away, but my words shall not pass away* (Matthew 24:35).

If God's Word was fallible—which means "liable to err," especially in being deceived or mistaken, and "inaccurate"—there could never be faith. Faith is tied to infallibility—which means "incapable of failing or erring," and "absolutely trustworthy or sure."

I said earlier that it is God's will to heal everybody. How could I make such a tremendous, blanket statement? I can say this because it is already recorded and documented in the Holy Bible, the Word of God, which is infallible, which is true, which cannot be questioned. It is already on record.

When the leper came to Jesus and said, . . . *Lord, if thou wilt, thou canst make me clean* (Luke 5:12), Jesus . . . *put forth his hand, and touched him, saying, I will: be thou clean. And immediately the leprosy departed from him* (Luke 5:13). He made His will known to them. He was **willing**. In Matthew 12:15, we read about Jesus that . . . *great multitudes followed him, and he healed them all* . . . Matthew 14:14 puts a motive behind His willingness: *And Jesus went forth, and saw a great multitude, and was moved with compassion toward them, and he healed their sick.*

After Jesus was lifted from this earth, the apostles that He had commissioned continued to carry out His work. We find this scene in Acts 5:16: *There came also a multitude out of the cities round about unto Jerusalem, bringing sick folks, and them which were vexed with unclean spirits: and they were healed every one.*

Many people just cannot believe that it is God's will to heal them. Many actually believe that God's will is for them to remain sick! One scripture that people apply negatively to their sicknesses is found in 2 Corinthians 12:7-9. It refers to Paul talking about a messenger of Satan having been sent to buffet him. He called it a thorn in the flesh. He said he sought God three times for God to take it away, but He didn't. God said His grace was sufficient for Paul. Many have supposed that the thorn in Paul's flesh was a physical affliction, though that is purely their supposition.

In the first place, Paul said he had this thorn in the flesh, this messenger of Satan, because he had received such an abundance of revelations from God. Paul shares the reason he was given that thorn in the flesh in the preceding verses, 2 Corinthians 11:23-30. Satan tried to keep him from sharing his revelations. It was to keep him from being exalted above measure. There are few people I know who have received such an exalted view of God's glory!

25

Why is it so hard to believe that Paul's thorn was not just what he said it was, a messenger or angel of Satan? It was a demon that opposed him wherever he went and that put him through numerous hardships. The reality of his faith in God to heal was demonstrated remarkably when he was bitten by a poisonous snake on the island of Melita (Acts 28:1-6). Paul didn't panic when the snake bit him. He did not call for a doctor, and he did not ask his friends to pray. Paul just shook the snake into the fire and went about his business. He was sure of God's will to heal and to keep him.

When God brought the children of Israel through the wilderness after they left Egypt, we have this tremendous statement of fact: *. . . there was not one feeble person among their tribes* (Psalms 105:37). It is true that Israel, as a nation, played a special part in God's world plan, and that they have enjoyed a unique position nationally, but I want you to know that God is no respecter of persons (Acts 10:34). He loves you and me just as much as He loved the Jews of that day. What He did for them, He will do for us. It is what He will do for the Church if we will just cut him loose to do it, if we just take the limits off of Him!

God's will to heal bodies has been especially stressed in this chapter, but God's will for us encompasses many other great blessings also. It encompasses total health, well-being, and total prosperity (3 John 2).

Many feel that it is God's will for them to be poor and in need and in want. I have known people who felt that there was something godly about worn-out shoes and an empty cupboard. If they don't have the faith to believe that it is God's will for them to have plenty, how can they pray in faith? Jesus said: *. . . I am come that they might have life, and that they might have it more abundantly* (John 10:10). Paul said: *But my God shall supply all your need according to his riches in glory by Christ Jesus* (Philippians 4:19). David said: *THE LORD is my shepherd; I shall not want* (Psalms 23:1).

David also said: . . . *no good thing will he withhold from them that walk uprightly* (Psalms 84:11).

God will grant us our desires in addition to our needs. *Delight thyself also in the LORD; and he shall give thee the desires of thine heart* (Psalms 37:4). *Many are the afflictions of the righteous: but the LORD delivereth them out of them all* (Psalms 34:19). He delivers us out of them **all**! He delivers us 100 percent, not 10 percent or 50 percent!

The Bible is filled with information that gives us the knowledge of the good things that God wants to do for us. It is Satan who has caused some scriptures to be twisted, misapplied, and taught falsely in our churches. It is so that people will not know that it is the will of God to want to pour out His blessings upon us in this day!

Another reason that some people cannot believe that it is God's will to heal or bless them is that they feel unworthy. They have committed some sin in the past, and Satan has kept them in bondage through guilt. It is true that we may not deserve God's blessings, but they are not given to us on the basis of our own worth. They are given to us on the basis of Christ's worth. As Christ bore our sins, He also bore our sicknesses.

Come now, and let us reason together, saith the LORD: though your sins be as scarlet, they shall be as white as snow; though they be red like crimson, they shall be as wool (Isaiah 1:18). Once God has forgiven us, we must forgive ourselves and not let guilt feelings continue to rob us of the good things of God.

Some years ago, there was a struggling young woman. She was barely surviving financially and was living paycheck to paycheck. She would run out of money before every pay day. At that time, it took three or four days for checks to get to the bank after they were cashed. She would write a check and then live in fear and dread that the check would get to the bank before she got there with her paycheck to cover it. For years, even after this lady was living on less of an emergency basis, she had an unreasonable guilt whenever she would write a check. "I just can't write a check," she confessed to a friend. "I feel so guilty." "Well," asked her friend, "is the check covered?" It was covered. This woman was living on guilt that had been carried over, which kept her from enjoying the convenience of her checking account. When she realized that she had money in the bank to cover her check, and realized that her feelings of guilt were not related to her real situation, she gained a new sense of security in writing checks.

There is no need to continue to feel guilty over things that have happened in our past and for which we have received forgiveness. We can go before God with a clean slate because of the forgiveness that we have in Christ. Our account, so to speak, will be completely covered. We can have a completely clear conscience. *As far as the east is from the west, so far hath he removed our transgressions from us* (Psalms 103:12). If we look in God's Word, and discover there is a place where we do not measure up, we can find forgiveness and come into alignment with God's Word. Sin brings doubt. A knowledge of forgiveness and cleansing brings faith.

THE wicked flee when no man pursueth: but the righteous are bold as a lion (Proverbs 28:1). It is God's will that we be bold as lions in claiming His promises. Whatever your situation or need, in whatever area of your life, God wants the very best for you. Just as Jesus answered the centurion (when the centurion's servant's need was presented to Him), He will say to you, **I will**.

Once we know that God is not only able but is also willing to meet our needs, we can go to the next step in cutting Him loose to do it. The next step is having an experience like the centurion had. He saw God in a way that was different than the way most of the other people there saw Him. He saw Jesus as He really is because he possessed a knowledge of authority and the chain of command. This knowledge of how things work spiritually is vital to our life and circumstances! With the use of this supernatural sense, he literally took the limits off of God. So can you!

HOW CAN WE SEE GOD AS HE REALLY IS?

The God we serve is a God Who knows no limits. This statement is so vital to achieving the answers to prayer and the abundance of life that God wants to give us that I want you to fix it firmly in your heart and mind. Say it out loud: The God we serve is a God Who knows no limits! We limit Him. We do not see Him as He really is. Pray this prayer with me: God, open our spiritual eyes so that we might see You as You really are.

All of us are born with five natural senses. We have the sense of smell, touch, taste, sight, and hearing. Man tries to understand God with these natural senses, but there is no way that you can reach God with your natural senses. You can enjoy His handiwork and His provision through these natural senses, but you can never reach God through them or see Him as He is.

Your senses are finite. They have limited capabilities. When we try to perceive God by these senses, what we are really doing is limiting Him by these senses. *But the natural man receiveth not the things of the Spirit of God: for they are foolishness unto him: neither can he know them, because they are spiritually discerned* (1 Corinthians 2:14). To comprehend God, man needs a new sense, a sixth sense.

The world has something they call the sixth sense or extrasensory perception (ESP). I'm not talking about that kind of sense or anything to do with thought transference or reading minds, etc. I am talking about a real sixth sense that we all can possess and which is even more crucial for us to have than any of our five natural senses.

To see God as He really is, to take the limits completely off of Him, we must have a sense that is totally unlimited. Such a sense would set God free to work for us—not according to our meager comprehension by our five natural senses—according to His unlimited capabilities:

1. With His limitless ability: . . . *able to do exceeding abundantly above all that we ask or think, according to the power that worketh in us*, (Ephesians 3:20).

2. With His limitless being: . . . *having neither beginning of days, nor end of life* . . . (Hebrews 7:3).

3. With His limitless creative power: And God said . . . *and it was so* (Genesis 1:6-7).

The reason that the God we serve is a God Who knows no limits is that He is the same God Who was in the beginning. He is the same God Who said . . . *Let there be light, and there was light* (Genesis 1:3). He is the same God Who created the universe, the planets, and the seas. This is our God. He is the same **I AM** God Who opened the Red Sea for Moses and the children of Israel to walk through, Who protected Daniel from being eaten by hungry lions, Who sent a raven to bring food to Elijah during a time of desperate famine, and Who slew the army of Israel's enemies with a hail storm so that His people didn't even need to fight the battle.

He is the same God Who resurrected Jesus from the dead. He is the same God Who poured out His Holy Spirit upon the disciples so that they might have power over all of the power of the enemy.

God, help us to see right now that You are the God Who is able to do miracles in our own life, in our own ministry, and Who is able to meet every need that we have—every need! We can have total care, total provision, total protection, total health, total peace, and total victory! That's the God we serve! If we could only see Him as the God that He really is. It is so essential to our experience and well-being to have that special sense, that sixth sense, in order to comprehend Him.

When Jesus spoke in parables, the ordinary, run-of-the-mill listener missed His point entirely. Jesus said of them: *Therefore speak I to them in parables: because they seeing see not; and hearing they hear not, neither do they understand* (Matthew 13:13). These people saw Jesus with their eyes. They heard Him with their ears. They tasted the fishes and the loaves that He multiplied. They missed the real point of His ministry completely because they were devoid of that spiritual sixth sense.

The centurion possessed such a sixth sense. When the centurion told Jesus about his paralyzed and tormented servant, Jesus offered to go to his home to heal the servant. The centurion's reply to this was that he not only was unworthy of Jesus coming to his house but that it was completely unnecessary for Him to come. There, on that street corner, he confessed Jesus as Lord. He told Jesus to speak the word only, and his servant would be healed. He said that he was under the authority of his leaders and also was a leader himself, with others under his authority. He said when he tells one of his soldiers to go, he goes. Whatever he tells his soldiers to do, they do it. He told Jesus that if Jesus would just speak, then whatever He commanded to be done would be done. He recognized that Jesus had authority over the sickness. Jesus marveled over this. He told the centurion that He had not found such great faith in all of Israel. The centurion had exceptional skill at utilizing a sixth sense. It is called **faith**.

Faith is not a natural force. It is a great inner knowing. It is not a thinking, not a believing, not a wishing, not a hoping, but a great knowing of Who God is, what He is able to do, and what He is willing to do. The centurion had this sixth sense—faith—in a way that no one before him had ever had. *When Jesus heard it, he marvelled, and said to them that followed, Verily I say unto you, I have not found so great faith, no, not in Israel* (Matthew 8:10).

The centurion had such an **inner knowing** of Who Jesus was, such a belief in His might, that Jesus said there had never been any greater faith. How could Jesus make that statement? Because He knew. He knew the centurion. He knew every person who had ever lived. How did He know? He was in the beginning and has known every human being who has ever existed. Jesus did not just begin when He was born in Bethlehem. That event only marked the beginning of his life on earth as a man.

John says this: *In the beginning was the Word, and the Word was with God, and the Word was God. The same was in the beginning with God. All things were made by him; and without him was not any thing made that was made. And the Word was made flesh, and dwelt among us, (and we beheld his glory, the glory as of the only begotten of the Father,) full of grace and truth* (John 1:1-3,14). The Word that became flesh was Jesus.

Jesus knew about the centurion and the centurion's level of faith because He was before the beginning. He **made** the beginning. He saw Abraham, Isaac, Jacob, Elijah, Moses, and Daniel. When He said to the centurion . . . *I have not found so great faith, no, not in Israel,* He knew what He was talking about. He was coming from the I AM position. He had always been and always would be. He was present with every saint through the ages, and He had seen the faith of Abel, Noah, and all of the great heroes of the Old Testament. Still, He said, I know what I am saying. There has never been any greater demonstration of faith than this centurion has demonstrated.

32

What was the centurion's demonstration? How could his faith be greater than the faith of Abraham, the "father of faith"? Think about it now. Here was a man, whose name was not even recorded in the Bible, yet Jesus said he had greater faith than any of the most revered of the great men who *are* named in the scriptures. How could He say that? **The centurion could see Jesus as He really is.**

Here stood the centurion with a tremendous need to present to Christ. His servant was at home, totally paralyzed and totally helpless. The need was great. If the centurion had not seen Jesus as He was, that need never could have been met.

Many people see Jesus as a philosopher or as someone with interesting or profound thoughts. They see Him as a good man, who lived many years ago and who did good works. Some may even accept or claim Him to be a prophet, but even that is not enough. You will never be able to break through to miracles with that comprehension or vision. You must see Jesus as He really is. He is more than a prophet. He is more than a philosopher. He is more than a good person. He is the very Son of the living God, with all of the power over the power of the devil.

Even people who had been with Jesus, who had witnessed His miracles, did not perceive Him as He was. If those who had walked with Him daily had been in the same situation that the centurion was in—even having seen the mighty miracles and knowing that Jesus was able to heal the sick—most of them would have said, Please come to my house. Let us, You and me, go together. When we get there, You can lay Your hands on him, and You can heal him.

Such a statement would, in fact, be a statement of faith. They might believe Jesus' Presence would heal or that His touch would heal, but look at the limitation that even that kind of statement would have placed on Jesus. It would have put the limitation of physical location on Him. It would also have put a limitation of method and of time on Him. He was bound by none of these limits.

If they added other qualifying statements, such as, You can make him better, or You can help him accept his condition, then that would have limited the need. Listen to the centurion's statement of faith that cut Jesus loose to work according to His unlimited capability and caused Him to remark on the centurion's faith and understanding. When Jesus offered to go to the centurion's home and heal his servant, *The centurion answered and said, Lord, I am not worthy that thou shouldest come under my roof: but speak the word only, and my servant shall be healed* (Matthew 8:8).

What the centurion was really saying to Jesus, in essence, was: When I look at You, and I see You as You really are, I see that it is unnecessary for You to come to my house. Why make that journey? Don't work for me according to my limited ability to understand. Do it according to Your own power. Simply speak Your Words into the air, and the wind—which is not limited by time or space—will carry the power of Your Words into my servant's body. Do it according to Your power. Speak. Stand right here, and speak the Word, and my servant will be healed.

Do you see what the centurion did with that one statement? He cut Jesus loose from the limits of time. He cut Him loose from the limits of space. He cut Him loose from the limits of need. He cut Him loose to work His unlimited work in His own unlimited way! The centurion's spiritual sixth sense was so acute and so positive that it took every limit off of God, and the miracle was done.

Wouldn't it be wonderful to have faith like that? You can have it. It is for you. You might say, but Brother Cerullo, I have tried to have faith. I have struggled and struggled to get faith. How can I get it?

The struggle to achieve faith, to have this sixth sense of inner knowing, is a very real and perplexing problem that people have. People struggle for years trying to get faith or to work it up or pray it down from heaven, etc. Perhaps that has been your experience in the past. If so, let us get that problem settled once and for all. No amount of struggling on your part will ever produce faith.

CHAPTER FIVE

MUST WE STRUGGLE TO PRODUCE FAITH?

Have you ever struggled to get faith? Have you cried and prayed and fasted and tried to have faith, yet somehow you fell short? Have you ever felt that, well, yes, the answer is out there, but it's just a little farther than you can grasp? It's too far to grasp, you think, but you say to yourself that if you could just struggle a little more . . .

Stop struggling! Faith does not come by struggling! It is a gift from God! We don't struggle to possess faith. It is a great inner knowing, an absolute confidence, that only God can give.

After a child is born, does he struggle to see? No. As soon as their little eyes can focus, they will follow the movement of their mother around the room or watch a hand moving near their face. Because a baby is born with eyes, they see. It is a normal result of their natural endowments. Does the baby struggle to hear? No. They are born with that hearing. A sudden, loud noise may make an infant cry. Hearing their father's voice will bring a smile to their face. They are not struggling to hear; they simply hear. Do they struggle to taste? No. Feeding time brings contentment because that milk tastes just right. A drop of medicine in the baby's water will bring an angry frown. They can taste. It is not something they struggle to do; it is just there. It is God-given.

35

So it is with all of the five natural senses that we have mentioned: sight, hearing, taste, smell, and touch. As those five senses are God-given, so is the power of the sixth sense, which we so vitally need—faith.

There is another thing that every person is born with that plays a vital role. It is a person's will. Each person has a will of their own. They can will to do this or do that, to obey God or to disobey. We can direct our lives by the choices we are able to make through our free will that God has given to us. Do you know that you can actually set that will to believe God if you choose?

When Lazarus died, Martha reproached Jesus for not having come earlier and healed her brother. *Jesus saith unto her, Said I not unto thee, that, if thou wouldest believe, thou shouldest see the glory of God?* (John 11:40). Jesus used a very interesting verb when He said, . . . *if thou wouldest believe* . . . The word *would* is part of the verb "to will." Jesus didn't say, If you <u>c</u>ould believe, He said, If you <u>w</u>ould believe. This indicates an act of the will!

Mankind has a will because we were created in the image of God. That image is not in how we look on the outside, how our eyes look, how our nose looks, how our cheekbones or any other part of our bodily form looks. It is in our spirit. God gave us control over our will. We can choose what to do.

Mankind abused this control by disobeying God. Adam took his will and submitted it to the influence and control of Satan. Because of this initial disobedience, humans throughout all subsequent generations have used their will in disobedience to God, doing those things that are contrary to God's will.

Salvation is all about God trying to get man to surrender his life—the control of his life (his will)—back to Himself. Man does this by believing and accepting Christ as Lord. When he does this, he is born again. He is a new creature in Christ. He becomes a spiritual being. *Therefore if any man be in Christ, he is a new creature: old things are passed away; behold, all things are become new* (2 Corinthians 5:17).

When a person is born again, they are born with a sixth sense, a gift of faith that is dropped into their heart. They have the ability to believe God. That sixth sense is just as natural to a newborn, spiritual Christian as the natural senses are to a newborn. That gift, and that ability, of the sixth sense grows and develops in us as Christians. It doesn't grow by our natural struggles to achieve it but by our will to continue to submit to God and to read, receive, and act upon His Word, to believe His Word. It was the gift of God that enabled Peter to see Who Jesus was.

Peter had his share of struggles. He had not understood the nature of Jesus or the nature of his calling on many occasions. He had made many mistakes and brought many rebukes upon himself. Yet God visited him and bestowed upon him the gift of the sixth sense, faith. In Matthew 16:13, Jesus asked His disciples, . . . *Whom do men say that I the Son of man am?* They answered that some said He was John the Baptist, some Elijah, and others Jeremiah or one of the prophets come back to life. He wasn't asking them who other people thought He was. He was asking them who *they* thought He was. *And Simon Peter answered and said, Thou art the Christ, the Son of the living God.*

Jesus then pinpointed how Peter had received this understanding: *And Jesus answered and said unto him, Blessed art thou, Simon Bar-jona: for flesh and blood hath not revealed it unto thee, but my Father which is in heaven* (Matthew 16:17).

On another occasion, when Jesus was walking with His disciples, they passed a fig tree that had no fruit on it, despite having leaves and greenery. It was not yet fig season. Jesus cursed the tree. The next day, as they passed the tree again, they discovered that the same fig tree had dried up from its roots. Peter called Jesus' attention to it. *And Peter calling to remembrance saith unto him, Master, behold, the fig tree which thou cursedst is withered away. And Jesus answering saith unto them, Have faith in God* (Mark 11:21-22). Translated literally, what Jesus was really saying was have the faith of God, or have God's faith, or have the faith that God gives.

Ephesians 2:8-9 points out that God is the giver of faith. *For by grace are ye saved through faith; and that not of yourselves: it is the gift of God: Not of works, lest any man should boast.* This applies not only to saving faith but to all faith. It is not of ourselves and never can be. It must, and it does, come from God. We can and do receive it as we come openly to Him and submit our will fully to His will and to His Word.

Hebrews 12:2 says: *Looking unto Jesus the author and finisher of our faith . . .* It is the Lord Who writes faith upon our heart and Who refines and finishes it. *So then faith cometh by hearing, and hearing by the word of God* (Romans 10:17). I need to point out, however, that there is a difference between believing and having faith. We can believe in something, yet not possess it. It is faith that appropriates what we believe. Faith is a fact, but faith is an act. It was this type of faith that the centurion had. He let his faith reach out and appropriate his miracle when he told Jesus to . . . *speak the word only . . .* God had given him that faith. He did not doubt that it would be accomplished.

Many people have said to me, "Brother Cerullo, don't you ever doubt?" Of course I doubt, but what I doubt are my doubts. I doubt my doubts because they are based only on human experience, human senses, and human limitations. Each of our natural senses at some time fails us. Our eyes may at times deceive us. Our nose might mistake one scent for another. A cold can rob us of both our smell and taste. Our ears don't always hear words just right. Our sense of feeling certainly is not infallible either. I would much rather doubt my own natural senses than to doubt the infallible, unchanging Word of God. If we are not careful, Satan can tamper with our natural senses or feelings, and we can be deceived.

Isaac went by his feelings when Jacob deceived him in order to receive the blessing that ordinarily would have gone to his older brother, Esau. Isaac's eyes were dim, so Jacob dressed in Esau's clothing. They had the smell of the outdoors on them. Jacob put the skin of a kid on his arms so that he was hairy to the touch, as Esau was. Isaac trusted his natural senses, and he was deceived. You can read about this in Genesis 27:1-29.

We must guard against trusting a natural sense over the Word of God. One is changeable and fallible; the other is forever unchangeable and infallible. I believe God because my faith comes from Him and is based on that which is far more trustworthy than any human instrument or tool or understanding could be. It is based on infallibility—God's infallibility.

SIX

HOW BIG IS GOD?

If Jacob was cunning in deceiving Isaac, think about how much more cunning the devil is in deceiving people! . . . *that old serpent, called the Devil, and Satan, which deceiveth the whole world . . .* (Revelation 12:9). Through deceiving our natural senses, he seeks to attack our sixth sense, faith. One way he does this is to bring negatives into our life so that we will only look at the negatives. If we do, then they will so fill our sight that we never will be able to see Jesus as He is.

Worrying and meditating on your problems is one of the greatest hindrances to faith. It is a spiritually blinding cataract that can keep you from seeing Jesus as He really is and from setting Him free to work miracles of deliverance and help in your life. If we keep our eyes on the problems or the difficulties surrounding us, there is no way that we can see how big God is and how mighty He is to meet those needs.

Not very long ago, this ministry felt led to take a giant step of faith. It was a step that was so giant, it seemed far greater than any challenge we had undertaken before. For years, I have been going to the far corners of the earth to conduct mass overseas crusades. As many as 300,000 people have attended a single service. Multitudes are healed of every disease and affliction imaginable, and even more are touched through these crusades.

The main thrust and the main burden of my heart in these overseas meetings has not been the crusades themselves but the very special meetings that are held during the day for the training and motivation of the Nationals. Long ago, God told me, "Son, build me an army." This army is comprised of dedicated men and women around the world who have learned the answer to the question, What must we do that we might work the works of God?

I teach them that miracles are not just for my ministry but must be an integral part of their ministries, to show the people of their countries that Jesus is alive and powerful today. As part of each School of Ministry, I have some of the key National ministers preach and pray for the sick in the great crusade services. I just stand back and pray quietly, and let them minister. What joy there is as they realize that the same Holy Spirit Who anoints Morris Cerullo also anoints them and uses their ministries to bring miracles of deliverance and healing! What excitement!

They leave those meetings transformed! I have seen it happen over and over again. I have seen men—who have usually preached to very small groups—soon have congregations of hundreds. People who usually were reaching hundreds soon are reaching thousands. When the crusade is over, the revival isn't! It is alive and flaming in the hearts and ministries of these men and women.

Our Schools of Ministry have enabled us to be welcomed into many countries where the Gospel is all but closed to traditional missionary activity. It is because of our interest in training the Nationals.

Over the years, the number of requests that have come in to invite us to hold these schools overseas have increased to the point where it would take me at least ten years to hold them all. However, the training is urgently needed now, especially in light of the tremendous population explosion all around the world. We are adding 76 million people each year to the roll of the unsaved (the lost). From 1976 until 2019, the world's population is expected to double to almost nine billion people! One-fourth (25 percent) of the world is now closed to normal missionary activity. To train and equip a missionary through the normal denominational channels costs almost $50,000 U.S. dollars. Over 100 million people are still without any scriptures written in their native language. In the year 1810, there were five missionaries. Today, there are more than 35,000, but only 28 percent are active in any kind of evangelism. This means that only around 10,000 are trying to reach over 6.6 billion heathen souls. Can you see why the need for trained Nationals is so overpowering?

I was thinking about this doubling and redoubling of the world's population and wondering how we could ever do the work that Jesus gave us to do. How could we go into all the world and preach the Gospel to every creature? Then God gave me a vision and concept. For the first time, I saw how this seemingly impossible task is possible. It can be done in our generation!

God led me to conduct Schools of Ministry where Nationals from all over the world could receive the training to bring their own country the message and the power of the resurrected Christ. This is not another Bible college or university or a school of theology. The School of Ministry is an intensified training for Nationals to learn to work the works of God effectively in their own countries.

The schools of ministry are for:

1. National leaders and ministers from all over the world to come for training, including North America. We need this NOW in North America as much as do the Nationals in Africa, Asia, and other areas of the world.

2. Christian laymen who realize that God wants to use them, even though they have commercial responsibilities in this world.

3. Those who feel called of God but who are frustrated at the theological and Bible school level of ministers' training. We equip them to take the offensive in spiritual warfare to conquer nations, cities, and villages for Christ.

4. Young people who have a definite call of God upon their lives. It is a tragedy that only 5 percent of the 60,000 students in Christian colleges and Bible schools in North America ever get to the mission field. If I can get these young people before they get into any other school, we can train them in the ministry of Christ and the disciples, through the Holy Spirit, and make them ready to come out of this boot camp training to become a vital part of the army of God.

For the first time, I could see how we could overtake the heathen! When God gave me this breathtaking concept, I knew that it was a big step. Circumstances would certainly have been frightening and would have disheartened me if I had allowed myself to look at them or to dwell on them. However, I knew that God had given me the key to meeting this great challenge. He also gave me added assurance during a special time of praying and seeking Him.

In my hotel room, while in prayer and just prior to speaking at a seminar that I was holding in Washington, D.C., God spoke to my heart with these words:

Do not look to the bigness of your need. Look to the bigness of your God. Your circumstances are hindrances to seeing My abilities! If you keep your eyes on your circumstances, the devil will use your circumstances to defeat you and accuse the Word of God—the written and the living Word. Your victory is in keeping your eyes on the bigness of your God and His ability. He has promised to take you step by step by step—not all at once, but step by step—and each step will be a miracle!

These words were so impressed on my heart that I had them put on a wall plaque for friends to hang on the walls of their homes to remind them every day: Do not look to the bigness of the problem. Look to the bigness of your God. In all of my ministry, nothing has strengthened me more than the comfort and daily, constant guidance that I receive as I repeat these words over and over again.

There are some people who are determined to look at their problems. There is no way that you can change the direction in which they are looking. They have looked at their problems for so long that their difficulties have become mountains in their sight, blotting out everything else. They can't see anything else. They can't speak about anything else. They can't even think of anything else. Often it seems that they must love their problems because they hold onto them so tightly. It is almost impossible to get such people to turn their sights on Jesus because they seemingly don't want to relinquish their troubles.

A woman called my office just a few days ago. She was in need of tremendous physical, emotional, and spiritual healing. Tearfully, she recited a long list of ailments that she had. She also recited a number of statistics on how many people went insane with her particular afflictions. This lady's afflictions were very real, but they were worsened by her preoccupation with her symptoms and how people treated her. One complaint she had was that she didn't get any sympathy from hospital and medical personnel. One got the impression that this lady was looking more for sympathy than she was looking to see Jesus. It seemed as though she was so wrapped up in her problems that she would not know how to function without them! After prayer, this woman was vigorously counseled to take her eyes off every symptom that she had and to think of and speak about only the goodness and greatness of God.

We are not Christian Scientists. We know that problems do exist and that people do have needs, and we do care. We also know that God is bigger than any problem and that if we will see Him as He is, He can take care of every problem and every affliction. We must learn to gird up our mind and bring every thought under subjection to Him and to think on those things that are edifying and helpful, not the negatives that Satan keeps sending us to keep our sight off the greatness of God.

Casting down imaginations, and every high thing that exalteth itself against the knowledge of God, and bringing into captivity every thought to the obedience of Christ;

2 Corinthians 10:5

Finally, brethren, whatsoever things are true, whatsoever things are honest, whatsoever things are just, whatsoever things are pure, whatsoever things are lovely, whatsoever things are of good report; if there be any virtue, and if there be any praise, think on these things.

Philippians 4:8

Certainly, one of the good and virtuous and right things that we should think on is the greatness of our God and what He is able to do and what He wants to do for His children.

SEVEN

WHAT THE CENTURION SAW

Certainly, the unnamed centurion in Matthew, Chapter 8, could not have been dwelling on negatives, or he never would have seen Jesus in such a brilliancy that his faith was ranked by Jesus to be above that of Abraham, Isaac, Jacob, or anyone else who had ever lived. He wasn't looking at any negatives to get that commendation! Neither was he looking with his natural eyes. If he had been, then the centurion would have only seen what every other person saw, and his servant may never have been healed.

What the centurion saw through his natural eyes was not the same thing that he saw with his sixth sense, his faith, his inner sense of knowing. When he told Jesus the condition of his servant, Jesus had graciously responded with the offer to come and heal him. That would have seemed like the thing to do to most people, but the centurion saw that this was a completely unnecessary act. *The centurion answered and said, Lord, I am not worthy that thou shouldest come under my roof: but speak the word only, and my servant shall be healed* (Matthew 8:8).

The reason that the centurion was able to make that statement with such faith is that he was not seeing Jesus merely as a tall Galilean who had just come down from the mountains with His friends to Capernaum. How did he see Jesus? Jesus was probably wearing the ordinary clothing of that period. He certainly was not wearing any type of military uniform or carrying any weapons of war. He was not wearing the insignia of some great military commander, but the sixth sense possessed by the centurion was able to discern that Jesus was the greatest and mightiest Commander, the most authoritative Person Who had ever walked on this earth.

In Jesus, he saw a parallel to his own situation, and he said to Him: *For I am a man under authority, having soldiers under me: and I say to this man, Go, and he goeth; and to another, Come, and he cometh; and to my servant, Do this, and he doeth it* (Matthew 8:9). **All truth is parallel.**

The centurion was a man with authority and with power. He had his uniform and his weapons. He had his unit of soldiers. He knew what his own ability and authority in the natural was. He was under the authority of the ruler of Rome, and by that authority, he was able to give orders that must be carried out instantly and obediently by those over whom he had been given authority. He could say to one man to go and take a message somewhere, and the man would go. He could tell another to give a report to the men in the frontlines of the battle—where it was risking the person's life to bring a report—and the man would report. He might say to an orderly to lay out his uniform, and the uniform would be laid out. Large or small, dangerous or mundane, whatever task he assigned would be carried out because of the authority that he had. He was a man of authority and was also under authority.

I have heard the story of an elderly man who lived some years ago in a one-store town, through which the highway ran. This man wore a badge that identified him as the local justice of the peace. Usually, this man didn't have much to do, just rest in his chair on the porch of the small courthouse, which also served as a post office. One day, as he lounged in his chair, the old man heard a great roar. He saw a big semi-trailer rig come barreling down the hill at a tremendous rate of speed. This man got up from his chair and walked out to the road. As the rig approached, he held his hand up in the air in a very commanding manner, though he stood scarcely five feet tall.

The truck driver saw the little, white-haired man, and he brought his rig to a screeching halt. When he got out of the cab, you could see that he was a big man, about 6' 2" tall and weighing about 250 pounds. He was at least twice the size of the little man who had stopped him. The truck driver began to apologize. He said, "I'm sorry! I didn't realize I was getting so close to town. I'm sorry. I promise I'll be more careful." The little man shook his bony finger at the big trucker and said, "I'm going to fine you $25 for speeding. Now either you pay up, or I am going to put you in jail!" The trucker followed the little man into the courthouse and meekly paid his fine. Then he climbed back into his truck's cab and slowly started to pull away.

Why did the trucker stop? The little man could never have walked out on the road and stopped that big rig. It would have smashed him flat. Why did the driver pay the fine? He easily could have whipped the old man with one hand. Why was he so submissive and obedient? He did it because of the authority the old man was under. That badge that he wore indicated that he was under the authority of the State of Nevada and that all of the resources of the state militia or National Guard were available to back him up. If that would not be enough, he had all of the forces of the Unites States behind him: the courts, Army, Navy, Air Force, Marines, etc. He was just a scrawny, little man, but he was a man under authority. When he spoke, the big, tough trucker had to listen!

The centurion was a man under authority, but when he looked at Jesus, he saw Someone Who was under a much greater authority than the authority that he was under. He saw One Who was under the authority of God Himself, the King of kings, the Lord of lords, the Ancient of Days, the Alpha and Omega, and the great I AM. He saw One Who was under the direct assignment and authority of

God the Father, Who had come to earth with this mission and this authority: . . . *For this purpose the Son of God was manifested, that he might destroy the works of the devil* (1 John 3:8). . . . *All power is given unto me in heaven and in earth* (Matthew 28:18).

He saw that Jesus was under a mandate from heaven and with the authority to carry out that mandate. He said, Jesus, you're just like me. I am under the authority of Rome, and I can command any one of the soldiers under me, and they will obey. I tell them to come, and they come. I tell them to go, and they go. You're here under authority, too, but it's a greater authority than Rome and a greater authority than any earthly authority. You are under the authority of Almighty God, and all of the forces of heaven are there to back You up. You can give orders, too. Your authority and dominion is not just over 100 men. It is over everything there is on the face of the earth. If You order the stormy wind to stop blowing, it will stop. If You say for the raging seas to be quiet, the waves will lie down and be quiet. If You say for a tree to be cursed and dried up at the roots, it's going to dry up and die. If You command a crippled arm to be stretched forth and healed, it is going to be stretched forth and healed. If You command a leper to be clean, as You did just prior to this meeting, that leper is going to be clean. You're under the authority of the God of heaven. You have His Name and His power to back up everything You say. If You will just speak the Word, my servant will be healed.

The centurion saw One with absolute authority and dominion over all of the power of the enemy, over all sin, over all sickness, and over all of God's creation. He saw beyond what Isaiah saw when he wrote: *IN the year that king Uzziah died I saw also the Lord sitting upon a throne, high and lifted up, and his train filled the temple* (Isaiah 6:1). He saw the authority that Paul had ascribed to Jesus, when he wrote a few years later, *For he* [God] *hath put all things under his* [Jesus'] *feet . . .* (1 Corinthians 15:27).

Before the death, resurrection, and ascension of Christ, he saw what Paul saw afterwards, when he wrote:

> *The eyes of your understanding being enlightened; that ye may know what is the hope of his calling, and what the riches of the glory of his inheritance in the saints, And what is the exceeding greatness of his power to us-ward who believe, according to the working of his mighty power, Which he wrought in Christ, when he raised him from the dead, and set him at his own right hand in the heavenly places, Far above all principality, and power, and might, and dominion, and every name that is named, not only in this world, but also in that which is to come:*
>
> Ephesians 1:18-21

The centurion knew beyond a shadow of a doubt that Jesus had full authority over his servant and over the paralysis that held him. And he knew that Jesus was willing to heal him, for Jesus had just said, *I will.* The sixth sense that the centurion had, when he told Jesus to speak the Word only, absolutely took every limit off of Jesus. It freed Him from every limitation of time—past or future—and left Him completely free to work NOW! It freed Him from every limitation of place—He didn't need to go to the centurion's house— He merely needed to speak the Word. There were no limits left. The limits were all completely taken off of Jesus.

A Roman soldier saw more than most of the devout religious leaders of that day. The religious leaders not only limited Jesus, but they had crucified Him because He invaded their nest. He tore down their traditions and exposed them as a generation of vipers. They saw Him only as a troublemaker. They tried to make Him out to be an imposter, an enemy. Jesus could have met every need that any one of those leaders may have had, if only they had seen Him for Who He really was! If they had seen His mission, His authority, His love, His willingness to meet them at their point of need!

Let us not limit Jesus ever again! Many who go so far as to acknowledge that He is the Son of God limit Him by what they can see or feel with the natural senses. They limit Him by the traditions of their churches and what they have been taught. They limit Him by seeing Him only as a philosopher or teacher. They believe He might even possess the Word of wisdom, but not of power. That brings us to the most crucial point of this entire message: How do YOU see God?

Do you see God as some far-off, unconcerned, undefined, mystical power? Do you see Him as the loving and personal heavenly Father? Do you see Him as too big or too great to worry about your individual need? Do you see Him not only as the Creator but as the One Who was so vitally interested in your need that He sent His only begotten Son here for the express purpose of meeting that need completely?

For God so loved the world, that he gave his only begotten Son, that whosoever believeth in him should not perish, but have everlasting life (John 3:16). . . . *I am come that they might have life, and that they might have it more abundantly* (John 10:10). *But he was wounded for our transgressions, he was bruised for our iniquities: the chastisement of our peace was upon him; and with his stripes we are healed* (Isaiah 53:5).

Do you see God as some outdated Force, irrelevant to today's needs, or as the One most completely concerned with your needs? Do you see Him as One Who is dead and Who is no longer able to do miracles, or do you see One Who is able to speak the Word only to your need—whatever that need may be—and know that it will be met?

I trust that by this time you are seeing Him as He really is. If you are not seeing Him as He really is, then I pray that you will fall on your face before Him, and ask Him to strip away the blindness from your spiritual eyes so that you can see—here and now, right at this very moment—how you can take the limits completely off of Him to meet your need. He has already spoken to every need that you have, and He did it two thousand years ago!

Because He has already spoken, there is absolutely no limit to what you can receive from His hand. Take the limits off of God. Let Him work for you. Invite Him to work for you. Do not limit God. Cut Him loose! Say: God, I loose You right now to work for me, not according to my limited comprehension of the past or even the present, but according to your unlimited capabilities. . . . *With men this is impossible; but with God all things are possible* (Matthew 19:26).

I expect great things. My eyes are not on my circumstances or my problems or my needs but on the bigness of the God Who is the Source of supplying and meeting those needs with His resources!

EIGHT

JESUS CHRIST HAS ALREADY SPOKEN TO EVERY NEED THAT YOU HAVE!

In all of the years that I have been ministering around the world, in all of the countries where I have been, I have never met one person who did not have a need of some kind. Whether it was a peasant or a queen—and I have sat with royalty in their palaces—everyone has needs, many of them desperate. Every day, I receive letters here at my office in San Diego, California, telling me of the most desperate needs that you could possibly imagine. People write to me with problems that are impossible to remedy in the natural. They are everything from terrible family situations, physical afflictions, emotional traumas, moral perversities, overwhelming financial burdens, and anything else that you could name. These are crushing burdens.

I want you to know that no matter what your need is, whether it is large or small, or whether it is a new problem or a longstanding problem, there is One Who stands beside you Who can and will meet that need in your life, if you will just see Him as He is. When you do, you will cut Him loose to do the impossible. You will cut Him loose to do that which you never dared to even hope could come to pass.

I command you today, everyone who is reading these words, in the Name of Jesus, cut God loose! Dare to take His Word, and stand upon it! Dare to say that what is impossible with man is possible with God. When the doctors tell you there is nothing more that they can do for you—that they can't heal you of the cancer, and they can't heal you of the gall bladder trouble, and they can't heal you of the heart disease, and they can't heal you of the sugar diabetes, and they can't heal you of the high or low blood pressure—I know that there is a Power Who will speak the Word, and you will be healed!

Cut God loose! Cut Him loose from every limitation! Cut Him loose from time! Cut Him loose from space! Cut Him loose from the situation of the impossible! Cut Him loose from the natural circumstances!

The centurion told Jesus, You don't have to come to my house. I'm going to cut you loose to act, not according to my ability to comprehend, but I'm going to cut You loose to perform according to Your capability. Speak the Word only, and my servant will be healed. . . . *Not by might, nor by power, but by my spirit, saith the LORD of hosts* (Zechariah 4:6).

It is not the work of Morris Cerullo but of the Holy Spirit. Wherever the Holy Spirit is allowed to operate, the wonderful, healing Presence of God flows like a mighty river. It is flowing even now. Whatever your need, put it in His hand. There is no limit to His power. He is unlimited. The only thing that can limit Him is you. Don't limit Him. Cut Him loose!

The centurion told Jesus to speak the Word. Jesus spoke, and the miracle was accomplished. Two thousand years ago, Jesus Christ spoke to your need! He spoke to your need when He was on Pilate's porch, and that angry mob cried out, Crucify Him! We will not have this Christ reign over us!

They led Him down a little, narrow staircase and strapped Him to a whipping post. The Roman soldier took that torture weapon—a whip with 13 leather straps embedded with dozens of pieces of metal and bone shards—and laid it again and again to the bare back of Jesus Christ. They laid a staggering thirty-nine stripes on His back! Those pieces of bone and metal would rip the flesh out of a person's back each time the whip was drawn back again. They did this to him thirty-nine times! They tore His back to shreds, until the words of the prophet Isaiah—written under the anointing of God seventy years before this experience took place—were fulfilled: *But he was wounded for our transgressions, he was bruised for our iniquities: the chastisement of our peace was upon him; and with his stripes we are healed* (Isaiah 53:5).

Two thousand years ago, Jesus Christ spoke to your need! I believe the cure for every disease and every affliction known to man lies in those thirty-nine stripes that Jesus took in his back. . . . *For this purpose the Son of God was manifested, that he might destroy the works of the devil* (1 John 3:8). With that crown of thorns on His brow, the blood spattering down His face, with His back torn to pieces so much so that His arteries were hanging out of His body, with the nails in His hands and the wound in His side, with the unfathomable weakness in His body as He walked toward Golgotha's hill—too weak to even carry His own cross—in this ragged condition, He spoke to YOUR need!

Though he were a Son, yet learned he obedience by the things which he suffered;
Hebrews 5:8

Who, being in the form of God, thought it not robbery to be equal with God: But made himself of no reputation, and took upon him the form of a servant, and was made in the likeness of men: And being found in fashion as a man, he humbled himself, and became obedient unto death, even the death of the cross.
Philippians 2:6-8

Two thousand years ago, Jesus Christ, the Son of the living God, spoke to your need. He spoke to that arthritis. He spoke to that cancer. He spoke to that fear. He spoke to that need. He spoke to every work of the curse. He spoke to it. He spoke to it in His own body on that tree. He carried every pain. He carried every weight. He carried every problem. He spoke to it. When He spoke the Words . . . *It is finished* . . . (John 19:30), He had fulfilled His mission to earth. He had paid the price for every sin. He had borne our sorrow. He had borne every disease. The Word destroyed every work of the enemy.

When we see Jesus as He really is—not only as the Speaker of the Word but the actual, living Word Himself—when we have that inner knowing that it is His will to meet our need, when we comprehend that not only need He speak the Word only but that He already has spoken to our need, the limit is gone. Our need is met. *NOW faith is the substance of things hoped for, the evidence of things not seen* (Hebrews 11:1).

The prayer of faith is tied to the evidence of what we see by the eyes of faith. This enables us to tie our prayer to that which is infallible—the promises of God. We see the fulfillment. We see the healing. We see the finances provided. We see the family difficulties solved, and the family healed. When we pray, we firmly believe and know because the sixth sense is working—faith! By faith, we see it done and continue, by the power of the Holy Spirit, to believe God's promises and speak according to what we believe, nothing wavering. Through faith we take every limit off of God. Nothing—I mean, absolutely nothing—is impossible for us to believe. We take our answer now. We take the limits off of God! Faith is a fact, but faith is an act.

It is important—before you take one step farther—that you act on what the Holy Spirit is stirring in your heart. Do it now. Do not delay. Otherwise, the whole purpose God may have for your life through the inspiration of this revelation could be lost.

A VERY SPECIAL SUPPLEMENT

Dear Beloved In Christ:

God has shown me that now is the time for us to take the limits off of our unlimited God. We must let Him work in our life, not according to our own abilities but according to His unlimited ability. We are going to see answers to prayer such as we have never seen before. For years, God has given me a special prayer ministry, and I want to make it available to you right now. Write down all of your requests, and mail them to me today. I will respond with a letter of ministry to your request.

Each request will go to our World Evangelism Chapel. Every Friday morning, members of my staff will join in prayer for these desperate needs to be met. They will also be placed upon our prayer altar, where staff and volunteer prayer warriors will storm the heavenlies for your answer.

Thousands of people have written to us to tell us how God has met their needs. Many times they have received a miraculous answer to prayer even before my prayer letter reaches them! We give God the glory.

You must have a part in this ministry and in these prayers. Together, we will take the limits off of God to meet those needs. It doesn't matter if they are mental, physical, relational, marital, financial, spiritual, or whatever else.

The last page of this book has been prepared especially for you. Fill it out with your needs and requests, and send it to me today. Turn right now to that special page. Be sure to write to me about each miraculous answer you receive as you take the limits off of God in your life, so that we can give God the glory and glorify His holy Name for answered prayer!

Morris

Morris Cerullo

ABOUT THE MINISTRY OF MORRIS CERULLO

Dr. Morris Cerullo, President
Morris Cerullo World Evangelism

Morris Cerullo's accreditation for ministry is in itself quite formidable: a divine, supernatural call from God to preach and evangelize when he was only fifteen years old, and over half a century of experience as a pastor, teacher, author of more than two hundred books, and worldwide evangelist.

Many honors have been bestowed on Morris Cerullo, including honorary doctorates of Divinity and Humanities, both by academic and spiritual leaders and heads of state around the world in recognition of his achievements and contributions to global evangelization.

Dr. Cerullo is respected and revered by millions around the world, including over one and a half million Nationals trained through Morris Cerullo's Schools of Ministry. His ministry outreaches include:

- **The Morris Cerullo _Helpline_ Program** – a major television, cable, and satellite weekly, hour-long, prime-time broadcast reaching out to hurting people in virtually every nation on Earth.

- **Schools of Ministry** – training national pastors, ministers, and lay people to reach their nations for Christ through mass evangelistic crusades.

- **The Elijah Institute** – The Elijah Institute: Dynamic training empowering national Christian leaders around the world to minister in the spirit and power of Elijah and raise up a network of Elishas to reach the world with the Gospel.

Dr. Cerullo has made a tremendous impact on the destiny of the nations of the world. He has sacrificially dedicated his life to helping hurting people and to train others who will take the message God has given him and train others.

We Care!

Dear Morris,

I am sending you my most urgent prayer requests.
Please pray for my needs:

_____

_____

_____

_____

_____

_____

_____

_____

_____

_____

❑ Enclosed is my love gift of $/£ _____ to help hurting people through the ministry of *Helpline*.

❑ Please send more information, including the benefits and resources I'll receive as a Circle of Hope member.

Name _____

Address _____

City _____

State or Province _____

Postal Code _____Country_____

Telephone (_____)_____

E-mail _____

Mail today to:
MORRIS CERULLO'S *HELPLINE*
U.S.: P.O. Box 85220 • San Diego, CA 92186
Canada: P.O. Box 3600 • Concord, Ontario L4K 1B6
Europe: P.O. Box 277 • Hemel Hempstead, Herts HP2 7DH